Black Daddy & Black Son Secrets (out the shower) Second Edition

By:Anthony Hawkins

ISBN:978-1-312-67844-6

Cover Art By Anthony Hawkins

Dedicated to the gay and lesbian community.

Prologue

It was a dark night on a friday and tall and dark and extremely handsome Lamar was driving down the highway with his girlfriends young 18 year old son Twan in the passenger side next to him,both of them silent as they drove down the highway.

Can you drop me off at my homeboy Roger house? Twan questioned Lamar as a child would their authority,his face very handsome and innocent.Dawg you should've been said something,we already on our way back to the house,you lucky i even felt like taking you to visit colleges man,i was tired as fuck today,your moms talking about she gotta work and shit,i had to work today too,but i still drove you all around,Lamar spoke to Twan with slight annoyance.

It's cool man,nevermind then,Twan spoke to Lamar softly.Man as a matter of fact you got gas money man,you can at least give me a tank of gas tho? Lamar spoke to Twan as Twan became silent.Dawg this is my moms car tho,Twan joked silently with Lamar as Lamar quickly pulled to the side of the dark road and stopped the car.

Why you stop man,you alright? Twan questioned Lamar with concern.Yea im alright,i just wanna know who you was talking to dawg? Lamar spoke to Twan angrily.What you talking about man? Twan questioned Lamar with deep confusion,Twan honestly not knowing what exactly it was that Lamar was talking about.

Nigga you know what im talking about,im talking about that slick smart shit you just said out your fucking mouth,talking about but this my moms car! Lamar spoke to Twan as his nostrils flared with anger.Man thats all,you tripping over that tho,i didn't think i said nothing that mad rude man,i thought i was joking? Twan spoke to Lamar as Lamar became even angrier.

Nigga get out the car,get the fuck out the car man! Lamar unfastened Twan's seatbelt and then getting out of the car and heading around to Twan's side to forcefully pull him out of the car by his arm.

Dawg,dawg you tripping man,what you doing all that for man?! Twan spoke to Lamar in an almost pleading voice as Lamar manhandled him out of the car and onto the trunk of the car with nothing but the dark open road and woods surrounding them.

Nigga shut the fuck up and bend your ass over man,we then did this before! Lamar ordered Twan as he held him by his arm against the trunk of the car.For what man,what you going do man? Twan spoke to Lamar with worry on his face.Dont worry about what im going do,just bend your ass over the fucking trunk,Lamar spoke sternly to Twan as Twan hesitated to comply with his orders.Nigga you think im playing with you right now man,huh,do you tho? Lamar spoke to Twan with a serious facial expression.Naw,i didn't say that,i just wanna know what you about to do man? Twan spoke to Lamar.

Since you cant pay gas you going sell some ass man,bend the fuck over! Lamar spoke to Twan,Twan still hesitating to comply with him.Look man,my bad for disrespecting you,i swear i wasn't trying be smart man,i was joking man,can we just go home now man? Twan spoke to Lamar as his face gave away fear and concern.

Nigga bend your ass over,and pull down your pants and underwear man! Lamar forcefully tossed Twan against the trunk of the car as Twan's face nearly hit the trunk.Im going give you a chance to do this shit yourself man,you want me to pull your stuff down or you can do it,what it's going be man,or I can leave your ass here in the middle of nowhere dude? Lamar spoke to Twan as Twan laid against the car trunk,his stomach pressed to the keyhole of the trunk as his rear end poked out a bit.

I got it man,just chill man,just don't try and leave me dude,thats cold man,Twan spoke to Lamar as he began to pull down his pants and underwear from his naked round posterior.Lamar began to help Twan pull down his pants and underwear and then began to pull down his own pants and boxers as his own rear end became exposed to the air outside.Lamar licked his hand and then began to massage his erect penis with it as he leaned Twan further over onto the car trunk,the flesh of Twan's face smushed onto the trunk while his posterior was still midair.

Lamar then gently slid himself into Twan's cavity as he bit his lip with lust,Twan gasping out as he felt Lamar enter him from behind.Ah man,go slow man! Twan shouted out in a light glitch of pain as Lamar began to glide himself back and forth inside of him from behind,Twan's head moving back and forth on the trunk of the car as Lamar continued to pound into his posterior from behind.

Yea nigga,i heard how you like dudes on that instagram shit,nigga whatever you post hit the streets dawg,yall stupid niggas nowadays need to learn that man,talking about you met a nigga on some gay app shit,since you love dick so much im gladly giving it to you,hope you enjoying it nigga,Lamar spoke to Twan as he penetrated his erect penis into him hardly,Twan maoning to the vibration of Lamar's swift thrusts from behind.

Take that dick boy,take that dick man,Lamar stroked himself into Twan in whispers of lust and pleasure as he pressed Twan's head further onto the car trunk.You want that nut nigga,tell me you want that nut dawg,say it,Lamar spoke to Twan.I want that nut dawg,Twan spoke out to Lamar in a strained voice as Lamar continued to penetrate him.Lamar forced himself into Twan one last time and then quickly pulled himself from out inbetween Twan's round posterior as he began to quiveringly ejaculate inbetween and on Twan's exposed posterior in pleasure,his moans loud and deep.

You good now man,get back in the car,Lamar spoke to Twan as he pulled up his own pants and underwear as if nothing happened.Twan leaned himself back up slowly and then began to slowly pull his pants and underwear back up over his sexually used posterior in silence as Lamar got back into the car.Twan then slowly headed back around to the passenger side of the car and then eased himself in with silence as he shut the car door behind him.

Lamar pulled off back onto the dark road after Twan was inside.

Chapter 1

Lamar continued down the dark road but then made a quick detour,and then pulling into a footlocker store as he began to park the car.

Stay right here man,i be back,Lamar spoke to Twan as Twan obeyed him in silence,Twan still thinking about what happened between them,the image of Lamar behind him playing over and over in his head as he sat in the car silently.Lamar was inside the footlocker store for about fifteen minutes and then finally came back out with a black and white stripy bag of newly bought shoes swinging from his fingers.

Lamar got back inside of the car and then handed the bag of new shoes over to Twan as if they were for him.What this for man,these mine or something? Twan spoke to Lamar with confusion.What you think,yea they yours man,sometimes its good for niggas to keep their mouth shut man,for real man,good things come to those who abide by the rules dawg,Lamar spoke to Twan as he began to reverse the car out of the parking space and then hitting the open road again while Twan looked inside of the footlocker bag to check out the new shoes he was gifted with.

Twan nearly looked in shock as he saw that the shoes Lamar had bought for him were shoes that were expensive and in style with men and young men alike,Twan nearly forgetting what happened between him and Lamar due to the materialistic items he was bought.

Lamar had bought Twan the shoes as a somewhat hush payment and secrecy bargain for what he did to Twan earlier,Lamar hoping the new items would keep Twan's silence and discreetness,and it did.

Your moms dont need to know what went down tonight man,that was between men man,we had a misunderstanding dawg,Lamar spoke to Twan as they continued down the road in the moving car.I feel you man,i got you,Twan spoke to Lamar,and then taking another silent and discreet glee look at his new shoes inside the bag.You sure you got me man,i got your word on that little homey? Lamar spoke to Twan again,wanting to make sure that Twan was discreet about their situation.What happened is squashed man,we all good man,Twan spoke softly to Lamar.My man dawg,Lamar spoke with satisfaction as his free hand rubbed the top of Twan's head playfully and affectionately as his other hand kept to the steering wheel of the car.

Twan and Lamar arrived home that night,and they both headed straight to sleep,tho Twan tried on his new shoes first before doing so.

The next week Twan was sitting silently at the dining room table as he marveled at his new shoes on his feet and drunk a glass of water.

Ay man,Twan greeted Lamar as he entered the dining room as well.Ay man,Lamar greeted Twan back,and then pouring himself a glass of water.Lamar headed towards the dining room table and then began to eye Twan silently.Your moms gone,you trying get something going? Lamar squeezed the bulge in his pants as Twan studied him silently.

Lamar moved closer to Twan and then pulled his thick penis from the hole in his boxers as he unzipped his pants silently,Lamar nearly waving his penis in Twan's face.We might get caught man,Twan spoke silently to Lamar as he looked at Lamar's penis and then Lamar's face in fear of being caught.Man stop bugging,put it in your mouth man,Lamar spoke silently and intimately to Twan as he moved even closer to him with his penis chucked into his hand.Man i dont know dawg? Twan hesitated to give Lamar oral sex.

Man you a bitch made nigga man,give me them fucking shoes back nigga! Lamar spoke to Twan.Man these my shoes man,i just got them man,you aint loan me these,you bought me these,you being petty now dawg,Twan spoke to Lamar,refusing to give up the new shoes he received from Lamar a week earlier.

Dawg you think im on joke time,you think im joking when i say i want them shoes back man? Lamar spoke to Twan.Man but dawg,you going be like that tho man? Twan spoke to Lamar with hesitation to give up his shoes.Man give them fucking shoes man,take these bitches off! Lamar began to force the shoes off of Twan's feet in anger as Twan struggled not to give them away.Get the fuck off me man! Twan shouted at Lamar as Lamar managed to pull one of the shoes off his feet,and then going for the other one.

Give these shoes nigga,i aint
playing,dont wanna suck a nigga dick
but you think you deserve new kicks
on your feet,nigga get outta here
with that shit man,that aint how shit
work dawg,give me these fucking
shoes,ungrateful ass nigga! Lamar
forced the other shoe from Twan's
feet as Twan struggled to get away
from his strong grip.

Fuck you man,i should tell my fucking
moms what you did nigga! Twan
yelled at Lamar in anger of losing his
shoes that he adored.Tell your moms
and watch me crack your whole

fucking face man,we taking it there
tho dawg,you a ungrateful nigga
man,after a nigga spend his money
on your bitch ass tho,fuck you too
man! Lamar spoke to Twan angrily as
he and Twan exchanged mean glares.

Lamar turned on the stove and then
sat the shoes on top of it,allowing the
fire from the flaming stove to engulf
the shoes in fire,the shoes burning
into a charcoal color and then
smoking in fumes of burning material
before Twan's very eyes.You fucked
up a good pair of shoes tho man?!
Twan spoke to Lamar as Lamar

smirked at him.These bitches burnt now dawg,Lamar tossed the shoes into the kitchen sink by the parts that weren't on fire and then ran water over them to put them out.Twan's eyes watched the wet and charcoal shoes in remorse as Lamar headed into he and Twan's mother Deedra's bedroom for his overshirt.

Im out man,if your moms come back before i get back tell her im hitting the block,Lamar spoke to Twan as he headed out the front door,slamming it behind him.Twan checked the shoes in the sink and checked to see if he was able to salvage something from them,but the shoes were severely burned and beyond repair.

Twan threw the damaged shoes in the trashcan by the burnt shoe strings and then sat back at the dining room table in anger of losing his shoes,but then texting back and forth with one of his friends to ease his rage.

Chapter 2

A few hours later Twan's mother Deedra came home,Deedra dropping her purse to the dining room table as she smelled the scent of something that was previously burning.Twan was it something burning in here,whats that smell? Deedra spoke to Twan as he exited his bedroom.

Lamar was trying cook and he burnt the shit,Twan lied to Deedra with a straight face as he fidgetted with his cellphone in his hands.Oh,whatever then,Deedra spoke to Twan and then heading into her room.Wake me up around like 7:00 pm if i dont wake up myself,i gotta be at work early today,and i hope i dont be doing too much because im cramping up,im on my period,Deedra spoke to Twan as she came back out her bedroom.Ew ma,i dont wanna hear about your period,Twan joked with Deedra as she snickered and then headed back into her bedroom shutting the door behind her as she got into her bed and fell asleep almost immediately still in her clothes.

Lamar headed back home after a few hours on the street,and then entered the house as he and Twan made eye contact with silent anger for a few moments.Your moms in there sleep aint she? Lamar spoke to Twan silently as Twan ignored him.Dawg it aint no need for the attitude man,all i did was ask you a question man,damn,Lamar spoke to Twan.

Yea man,she sleep,Twan spoke hesitantly to Lamar with an attitude.Im going let her sleep up in that joint and chill on the couch then,Lamar spoke out.Lamar sat himself down on the sofa and then turned the televison set on and then put the volume on medium as he began to watch it silently to himself,bags in his hand,bags that he soon sat beside the sofa.

Here man,i aint no trifling nigga,so you can stop your bitching,Lamar slid a box of shoes from one of his bags across the floor to Twan as Twan nearly gleamed to see what was inside the box.Twan pretended as if he was unfazed by the box of shoes as he picked them up from the floor and peeped inside.Twan saw that the shoes were the same size and brand of shoes that Lamar had previously ruined and burned in the kitchen earlier in the day,he was in glee once again,but acted if he wasn't,giving Lamar an unfazed and slightly angered facial expression as he held tightly to the box of shoes in his hand.

Tsk,nigga stop acting like you aint glad as fuck i bought you them shoes back,Lamar sucked his teeth at Twan and then began to watch the tv set once again as he leaned back onto the sofa.

The hours blew pass in no time,and soon Deedra was waking up for work,her body dressed in the same clothes she wore to sleep as she headed out into the living area with Twan and Lamar,Lamar sleeping on the sofa as Twan texted on his cellphone at the dining room table with his new pair of shoes resting in his lap.

Babe wake up,you feel like driving me to work tonight? Deedra woke Lamar up as Lamar's weary eyes opened in anger.What the fuck man,why you waking a nigga up for man? Lamar spoke to Deedra with annoyance.I want you to drive me to work,Deedra spoke to Lamar.Man naw,im tired man,you better get your ass to work before it get late,let me get some sleep man,Lamar spoke to Deedra,and then heading back to sleep on the sofa as Deedra sucked her teeth angrily at him.

Twan your little cousin Mark coming over here this weekend to spend the night,you know how he crazy about you,so try and find some games for him to play before he get here ok,just do me that favor,Deedra spoke to

Twan.Alright,i got you,you know thats my little dude,Twan spoke to Deedra as she headed to the dining room table to grab her purse and car keys and then heading out of the front door as she locked it,Twan then heading into his bedroom,closing himself inside.

The next day Twan woke up to Deedra and Lamar arguing loudly in the other room,Deedra up close and personal in Lamar's face as he was up close and personal in hers.

Nigga you act like you wanna hit me,do what you gotta do nigga,whats up?! Deedra yelled in Lamar's face as she welcomed him to hit her.Get the fuck outta my face yo,im telling you man,you better get the fuck outta my face! Lamar yelled back at Deedra,both of them having a screaming match.

Deedra reached up to hit Lamar,but Lamar quickly grabbed her hand and began restraining her as she tried to break free of his strong grip,Deedra cursing and swearing loudly while still in his grip.Get the fuck off of me,you cheating with bitches,but cant admit the shit,you can cheat,but just dont let me catch you,i saw your fucking phone,got numbers all up in that motherfucker! Deedra yelled angrily at Lamar.

Man stop fucking tripping Deedra,you acting real stupid now man,that shit aint rolling with me,you over here popping off over a few numbers tho,leave that shit to the birds,it aint that serious man,stop fucking showing your ass! Lamar yelled at Deedra as he kept a tight grip on her.

Ay Twan come and get your moms dawg,she acting fucking stupid right now,take her in the room and calm her down,im about bounce for minute! Lamar spoke to Twan as Twan entered the room to see what all the commotion was about.Twan quickly grabbed Deedra to calm her down while she still tried to assault Lamar while in Twan's grip.Come on ma,stop it man,calm down,he aint worth it,let's go in your room,Twan tried to soothe Deedra's anger as she screamed and yelled at Lamar,and then managing to break free from

Twan's grip after Twan loosened it on her promising him she was calm.

Dirty ass motherfucker! Deedra started to hit Lamar in his chest as Lamar stood unfazed by her blows.Chill the fuck out man,i aint with all that shit today! Lamar gently shoved Deedra into Twan's arms angrily as Twan caught her just in time.

Man you aint have to push her like that,you couldn't just grabbed her hands,it's not like you aint cheating man,Twan spoke to Lamar.Nigga shut the fuck up man,im out! Lamar spoke to Twan and then heading out of the front door,letting the door slam behind him,leaving Twan inside the house with an angry Deedra.

I swear im going fuck him up man,he going stop fucking playing with me,he cheated before and i forgave his ass,and then he cheated again after that and i forgave his ass,niggas dont know when they got it good! Deedra spoke to Twan in anger of Lamar's infidelity.Twan eventually managed to get Deedra to calm herself,Deedra falling asleep afterwards.

Deedra gave Lamar the silent treatment the next few days,but finally began to speak to him again a bit at a time.

Chapter 3

It was now the weekend,and Twan was awaiting the arrival of his younger 7 year old cousin Mark,while Deedra prepared herself to go grocery shopping,Lamar sitting on the sofa watching the television set after getting home from work.

Remember to find Mark some games to play,you gotta keep that boy busy,you know how he is,Deedra spoke to Twan as Twan stood near the dining room table.Man lock that little nigga in the closet somewhere when he get here man,he going be here all motherfucking weekend long,Lamar spoke out loud.Lamar dont act like a ass when that boy get here,it's only for the weekend,and Twan make sure he ok and he in bed around 9:00 pm,Deedra spoke to Lamar and Twan,and then leaving them home alone as she went out shopping.

Young Mark arrived just ten minutes after Deedra left,Twan welcoming him in with an embrace as Mark hugged Twan with excitement and joy.Hi Lamar,Mark spoke timidly to Lamar as he came inside and sat at the dining room table with Twan.Whats good little dude,i hear you going be here all weekend? Lamar spoke to Mark.Yes sir,Mark spoke to Lamar.

Alright man,let's go play some games on the ps3,Twan spoke to Mark as Mark gleamed in childlike excitement in response.Yes! Mark spoke out in gleam as he and Twan headed into Twan's room to play video games.About thirty minutes later Mark had fell asleep on Twan's floor,Twan covering him with a warm blanket and then closing him silently inside his room as he tiptoed back into the living area to take a hot shower.

Twan caught Lamar at the front door silently arguing with an unknown female just as he was about to enter the bathroom,tho Lamar and the woman were arguing as if they did know one another,and it was as if the woman was scolding Lamar about something.

Lamar im getting tired of your bullshit nigga,tell that bitch you got somebody and call it a day,i aint no side bitch,and im not going keep on playing no side bitch for no nigga! Twan heard the woman speak to Lamar.Man you coming to my house tho,where i lay my head man? Twan then heard Lamar speak back to the woman.I dont give a fuck where i came,you need to let your woman know you fucking me and that we been fucking for the past few months! the woman spoke to Lamar as Lamar became angrier and angrier.

You is a punk Lamar,you a real bitch nigga,the woman then spoke to Lamar,Lamar then slapping her across the face,the sound of Lamar's hand making impact across the womans face echoing.Fuck you Lamar,fuck you nigga,i spit on your shit motherfucker! the woman screamed at Lamar outside the front door,and then spitting on Lamar's shirt angrily.

Bitch you outta your fucking mind man?! Lamar headed out the front door after the woman after being spit on,the door closing shut behind him before Twan could see what was happening outside of it,tho Twan could hear the woman being punched repeatedly as she screamed and as Lamar cursed at her.

Twan quickly headed to the window to see what was happening,but all he saw was a quick glance of the womans slightly bloody lip as she cursed and headed away from the house while Lamar cursed back at her in anger,Twan was somewhat scared,he had never seen Lamar that angry before.

Twan quickly headed into the bathroom as he heard Lamar entering back into the house from his violent and heated situation with the unknown woman,Twan not wanting

Lamar to know that he was listening in to the whole thing.

Twan stripped himself of all of his clothes as he let them fall to the bathroom floor in light thumps,and then he stepped his naked body into the bathtub as he turned on the showerhead.The showerhead rained down hot and steamy water onto Twan's naked body as Twan began to soap himself up under the water beating against his body.

Twan washed himself thoroughly for
at least twenty minutes while Lamar
took a shower in the other bathroom
down the hall from the one Twan was
using,Lamar feeling dirty and
disrespected after being spit on by
the unknown woman awhile ago.

Twan showered for three more
minutes and then stepped himself
out of the shower as he placed a
short white above knee length towel
around the waist of his naked
body,and then stepping his feet into
shower shoes as he exited the
bathroom into the living area,the

open air whisking against his exposed flesh.

The opening bathroom door down the hall from where Twan stood exposed quickly caught Twan's attention as he watched Lamar exit the hot and steamy bathroom in nothing but a short white above knee length towel as well,Lamar's muscular built body just as radiant and smooth as Twan's,his wide shoulders and muscled arms and bulging pecks catching Twan's attention in an unusual way.Twan had never been attracted to

Lamar,even when Lamar forced himself upon him sexually that dark night on the side of the highway in the woods on the trunk of the car he never once thought of Lamar sexually,but seeing Lamar practically naked for the first time aroused Twan a bit,tho he didn't let it show.

Lamar saw Twan standing naked in nothing but the short white above knee length towel around his waist and the shower shoes on his feet in the middle of the hallway as he made eye contact with Twan as well,Lamar examining Twan's body completely and tensely as they both stood down the hall from each other,their eyes still locking,Lamar pretending to look away from Twan but then taking more glances at him.

What you was in the shower man? Lamar spoke to Twan slightly nervously and tensely,Twan sort of stunned that Lamar was showing a more vulnerable side to him,tho Lamar continued to hold onto his bad boy image.

Yea,i was in there for a minute,im just getting out tho,Twan spoke silently to Lamar as they continued to stare at each other,their conversation slightly intimate in tone.Check that closet in the hallway right next to you,Lamar spoke to Twan,Twan not having a clue to why he told him to do so.For what tho? Twan questioned Lamar silently.Man just check it man,Lamar ordered Twan again.Twan slid open the hallway closet as his eyes examined a bright pink baby blanket and a bright baby blue baby blanket both sitting at the top shelf of the closet,his eyes staring back at Lamar with confusion.

What the fuck dude,what you wanted me to see? Twan spoke to Lamar.The baby blankets nigga,i bought them when i first met your moms,i had forgot what gender she told me you was,you was like 4 i think,so i bought two blankets,a female one and a male one,but your moms told me to throw them joints away because she was mad i forgot,so she aint want you to have neither one of them joints,Lamar spoke to Twan almost warmly.

dude you going show me baby blankets you bought for me when i was little tho? Twan half smirked at Lamar.Dawg that shit aint funny,i was trying have a fucking moment with your ass man,but you acting all simple and shit right now,like i said before man,you a ungrateful ass little nigga man,Lamar spoke to Twan in a bit of annoyance.My bad dawg,stop tripping,Twan spoke to Lamar.

So what made you wanna lay up with other niggas tho man? Lamar spoke to Twan.I did,i just knew i liked dudes man,aint nothing else to it,Twan spoke to Lamar as Lamar got closer.I mean,i like fucking dudes,and making them suck my dick,but that don't make me gay tho,Lamar spoke to Twan in denial as Twan looked at him as if he were stupid.What position you like,you like when them niggas getting from the back or when they tearing it up from the front? Lamar spoke to Twan with a smirk.

Man stop playing man,you trying be funny now dawg,Twan spoke to Lamar with no humor at all.Im just saying man,you like when they go deep in here? Lamar moved his hand upwards along Twan's abs,meaning Twan's smooth stomach,more so Twan's inner stomach.Man you trifling dawg,and for that shit you did that night man,i aint forget that shit man,you foul dawg,Twan spoke angrily to Lamar.Man i was trying man you up cuz,niggas need guidance my dude! Lamar spoke to Twan in a lie that both Twan and himself could see clearly.

Naw dawg,more like you was trying get a nut dude! Twan spoke to

Lamar.Nigga you gay anyway nigga,stop acting like you was fazed by that shit man! Lamar spoke to Twan.So what man,that didn't mean i wanted your fucking dick in me dawg! Twan spoke to Lamar.Look at you getting all mad and shit dawg,you dont know if you wanna duke it out with a nigga or get fucked nigga! Lamar spoke to Twan as he moved even closer to him.

Back the fuck off me nigga,im not with that shit man! Twan spoke to Lamar in deep confusion.Twan slightly feared he was even more

open to Lamar's domineering
sexuality and violence due to their in
home private and practically naked
predicament,but he still chose to
standup to Lamar.

Make me back the fuck off then
dude,do something? Lamar spoke to
Twan.Hit me nigga,i dare you to hit a
nigga,im waiting son? Lamar poked
his handsome face out boldly to Twan
as he awaited Twan to throw the first
punch,Their faces nearly touching as
their exposed deep smooth chocolate
brown colored flesh and exposed
chests and navels and short white

towels and thighs and feet nearly touched as well.

Man i aint trying fight you man,fuck you,Twan spoke to Lamar,Lamar standing taller than him.What nigga,i fucked you in the ass,and what nigga?! Lamar began to tease Twan about their night on the highway in a bad way,Lamar knowing he would cause Twan's anger to flare.

Twan then punched Lamar directly in his strong jaw as Lamar shook it off with ease and without damage and then wrapped his arms tightly around Twan to wrestle him roughly and strongly to the floor with him,both Twan and Lamar in a heated tussling match that soon turned into an intimate and heated fit of growing passion as they tussled in nothing but their short white towels on the floor.

Lamar placed Twan in a tight strong grip inbetween his strong toned legs as Twan struggled to get free.Suck that dick nigga! Lamar placed Twan's mouth onto his growing very thick penis as Twan Tried and managed to move his face and mouth away from it in anger and a dormant deep sense of passion.Suck that dick nigga! Lamar forced his penis back into Twan's mouth again,this time Twan seeming as if he weren't struggling as hard to get away this time,Twan seeming as if he was allowing Lamar's erect penis to invade his warm and wet mouth.

Twan could no longer hold onto his opposition to Lamar's sexual advances because he was becoming just as aroused as Lamar already was,and a part of him hated himself for it,but he and Lamar were deeply in the heat of the moment.

Twan guiltily and lustfully shoveled Lamar's hard and dark penis into his mouth in one huge gulp as he began to deeply suck and devour Lamar's penis whole as Lamar moaned out in pleasure.Twan's mouth was bloated with Lamar's penis as he tasted Lamar intensely in his sexual flavor,Lamar pushing his slightly exposed crotch and penis upwards as Twan pushed his mouth and head downwards.

Suck on that dick nigga,thats right man,let that freak out nigga,little nasty ass little nigga man,im nasty too,Lamar moaned out deeply to Twan as Twan started to suck and blow his inner jaws onto his penis in deep gagging and popping sounds that echoed throughout the living area as Lamar caressed and pushed his head down further onto his hard huge penis.Twan's towel covered crotch area grinded onto the floor lustfully as Lamar's penis lustfully grinded into his mouth from under his own towel as squishy and gurgling sounds vibrated from their passionate and intense oral sex,the huge print of Lamar's big hard erect penis showing from the inside of Twan's gulping mouth and jaw outline as he gagged on it fiercely.

Twan popped Lamar's penis out of his smooth wet mouth and then began to glide his tongue up the thick strong shaft of it and then all the way to the top as Lamar shouted out in thrilling pulsating pleasure,Twan enjoying it as well,his own penis being sexually stimulated by his thrusting movements of his crotch and the presence of Lamar's hard muscled body.

Suck that dick baby boy,suck on it dawg,i know thats right nigga,do that shit man,fuck yea man,you cool little dude,i aint going hurt you baby,i aint going hurt you,and you nice and sloppy with that shit dude,h'm nigga! Lamar moaned out in deep pleasure of Twan's fast bobbing head on his erect penis as Twan stroked it as well with one of his soft and smooth hands,Lamar being even more sexually thrilled that Twan was being submissive to him and allowing him to explore him sexually.

Make that dick bust baby,make it bust little dude,bust that shit in your mouth baby! Lamar squirmed intensely in pleasure as Twan gulped his penis back and forth,smacking his full lips on it each time he swallowed it whole again,Lamar ejaculating first term ejaculation into Twan's mouth as his throbbing and stimulated and swollen with semen penis prepared for the entire full second term load that could soon be in Twan's warm welcoming mouth.

Twan wobbled Lamar's huge hard and slinky penis in his hand and then took his mouth down onto it slow as Lamar moaned,Lamar feeling his ejaculation circulating into the very tip of his throbbing penis as he tried his best to keep it in,Lamar not wanting he and Twan's sexual activities to be over yet,he wanted more,and wasn't shy about asking.Let me get some of this dude,shit is phat too,i want my hot nut up in there,Lamar moaned out to Twan in a whisper as he squeezed and caressed and played around with Twan's naked round smooth plump buttocks under the rear of Twan's short towel.

Get up for a minute baby,Lamar spoke to Twan as he eased himself up a bit while Twan eased up a bit as well,both of them preparing to assume another sexual position together,Twan a bit shocked at Lamar calling him baby,but was too aroused to think too much on it,Lamar and Twan both being affected by the strong hold that passion and lust brought to the table sometimes momentarily and sometimes forever.

Chapter 4

Man little dude in the other room man,dude might catch us man,Twan spoke to Lamar in deep moans and breaths of lust.Man that little nigga sleep man,he aint catching nobody dawg,just get ready for that dick man,alright,Lamar moaned back to Twan in deep breaths of lust himself,his big strong hand caressing Twan's soft cheek.

But man,Mark right in there tho man,Twan spoke to Lamar very silently.Man your little cuz in there knocked the fuck out dawg,he dont know whats going on out here man,you aint going pull no fast one on me now man,not when you got my dick all on brick dude,our flow was going good,stop tripping little homey,alright,Lamar spoke silenty to Twan in a low moan of sexual excitement that needed to be fulfilled.

But dawg? Twan spoke to Lamar as Lamar became annoyed.Nigga shut that shit up,lay down on the carpet dawg,Lamar forced Twan to the carpet with his strong grip as Twan fell to the small area rug on his back as Lamar began to hover above him.

Lamar watched Twan's nude short white towel covered waist sculpted body in the lustful thoughts of what he would do to it as he slid his own short white towel from around the waist of his hard strong and muscular nude body and began to masturbate his thick erect penis after wetting it with his tongue as Twan still laid beneath him in sexual convulsions.

Im not with this no more man,this
aint cool,let me up man,Twan spoke
to Lamar in a silent moan of pleasure
and guilt all at the same time as
Lamar ignored his guilt filled words
only,but not his toned body.Im going
tell my moms man,let me up man,im
going tell her what you be doing to
me,Twan spoke in a near whine of
passion and guilt once again as Lamar
smoothly glided himself into Twan's
naked body as he unwrapped Twan's
towel from around the waist of his
naked exposed body,Twan gasping in
pleasure as he felt Lamar's huge erect

penis smoothly slide into him in a warm sensual union of both their naked flesh joining together.

Twan felt a different kind of feeling this time as he felt Lamar deeply inside of him,it wasn't like the last time back at the dark highway,but a new sensual and pleasurable sensation of mild consent and heated passion,a part of him wanting Lamar to sexually take him on the area rug,but an innocent childlike part of him screaming inside for Lamar to stop,but Twan's young matured and

adult sexuality and urges discreetly
screamed for him to keep on.

You talking about you going tell your
moms,little snitching ass nigga,tell
her this,h'm,Lamar shoveled his hard
penis further into Twan's cavity as
Twan moaned out,Lamar then
smoothly rocking himself back and
forth on top of Twan in pleasure of
their bodies lustfully colliding flesh to
flesh.Twan mentally didn't want
anything sexual to transpire between
him and Lamar but he couldn't stop
his body from naturally responding
physically to what was happening

down below,Lamar's penis massaging him deeply inside in sexual thrill in the right places.

Twan and Lamar's naked skin worked smoothly together in a hot embrace as Twan moaned in lust,Lamar biting down on his lip in lust each time he heard Twan moan out,Twan's moans arousing him even more,almost as much as Twan's naked flesh.

Twan felt open and exposed but sexually stimulated as Lamar continued to shove his penis back and forth into his nude body in grunts of lust.You going get that dick man,huh,huh baby boy,you going get that nut up in you? Lamar spoke silently to Twan in a moan of lust as he then kissed Twan passionately on the lips as if they were lovers instead of he and Twan's mother Deedra.

Give me them lips nigga,Lamar began to deeply and lustfully kiss Twan all in his mouth as Twan tried to resist him,but failing to do so completely.Twan tried to push Lamar off of him,but Lamar forcefully pushed himself further onto Twan as

he began to stab his erect penis
faster and harder into Twan's body as
their naked bodies bounced up and
down ferociously on the rug in sexual
friction,Twan crying out in pleasure
and guilt.Twan then tried to move
himself sideways hoping for Lamar to
fleshly disconnect from him,tho
Lamar kept himself deeply inside him
even from the side,Lamar then lifting
Twan's leg a bit by his exposed thigh
as he smoothly and forcefully
injected himself into him
continuously and mercilessly as Twan
felt his inner fleshly walls being

plucked and served in the right and most pleasurable nerve spots.

You trying get away tho man,huh baby,you trying get away from that big dick in you,it feel good little dude,huh? Lamar spoke to Twan in a whisper of lust as he kept giving Twan his pelvis and penis whole as Twan laid beneath him in an agony of deep pleasure and thrill and whines of ecstasy,Twan's inner loins heating up in throbbing excitement and pleasure with every thrust of Lamar's naked waist and penis.

Twan held tightly to Lamar's strong forearms as Lamar began to do sexual push ups inside of him,Twan's voice vibrating to the thrusts Lamar gave him long and hard,Twan's loins beginning to throb and wet just as Lamar's did,Twan was unable to keep his moans and heavy breaths of pleasure to himself as he and Lamar's nude bodies violently but sexually jerked up and down and back and forth on the rug together.

Lamar could feel himself coming closer and closer to ejaculation as he continued to plunge himself back and forth into Twan in intense throbbing sensation. Twan had completely given into the basic human sexual carnal instincts as he enjoyed all that Lamar was doing to him.

Man im about to pee man! Twan lied to Lamar in a dragged out pleasure filled voice that sounded as if he was close to a climax of sexual peek, Twan hoping Lamar would stop, tho Lamar kept going, Lamar knowing he was lying. Nigga you aint about to pee, you

about to get one off,me too nigga,let
that shit out man,Lamar moaned
back to Twan in lust.

Lamar then squashed and crammed
his naked flesh onto and into Twan's
naked flesh in a deep sensual circular
motion of their naked hot bodies as
their bodies were fleshly locked
tightly together in a pit of their
chocolate colored flesh on the
rug,their smooth lips nearly
stuttering in the pleasure they both
felt deeply.

Lamar's naked pelvis gave Twan's naked pelvis five more thrusts of sexual pleasure as Twan grabbed tightly to Lamar's strong and hard round flexing buttocks and then Lamar quickly but smoothly slipping his erect and intensely throbbing penis out from inbetween Twan's tight inner contracting muscles and fleshly tunnel as he began to intensely and pleasurably and loudly ejaculate into and onto Twan's naked body as Twan exploded in an intense and explosive and very pleasurable orgasm of his own as he laid to the rug.

Lamar's hot semen partly flooded into Twan's naked body as most of it nearly drowned Twan's naked body and abs and crotch in its hot thick white substance as Lamar's own naked body towered above Twan's in moans of deep satisfying pleasure that escaped from Twan's lips as well. The huge mushroom shaped tip of Lamar's still throbbing penis was wet with his hot semen as Twan was wet with the same semen all over his naked body as he panted back and forth below Lamar.

Chapter 5

Twan and Lamar heard tiny footsteps approaching as they panted heavily together,and then quickly turned to the sound.

Twan and Lamar were now looking at what caused the sound of tiny footsteps,and it was young Mark,his eyes staring at both of them in childlike curiosity as they both were in their nakedness,Lamar's naked body on top of Twan's naked body.

Why is snot coming out of your weewee? Mark spoke to Lamar with concern,Mark too young to understand what it was exactly that was erupting from Lamar's penis onto Twan's nude body.Man go back in the room little dude,me and your big cousin was just playing,thats what come out your weewee when you like somebody,me and Twan like each other,you going know when you get older,stay outta grown people business boy,Lamar spoke to Mark as he quickly stood his naked body up from Twan's semen soaked naked body that laid beneath him,guilt on both he and Twan's faces.

Just go in the room man,i be in there alright,close your eyes man,Twan spoke nervously to Mark as he stood to his feet naked and his exposed abs drenched with Lamar's semen as it smoothly rolled down his smooth shiny abs like lava.

Young 7 year old Mark was very curious about what exactly Twan and Lamar were doing,Mark catching them at the sexual climax of their passionate sex fling together,Mark knowing that there was something more and unknown to him that they weren't telling him,the way how some children became suspicious of the realness of Santa Claus.

Man go in the room,hurry up,stop being nosey,and dont say nothing either man,Lamar ordered Mark sternly but nervously and guiltily.Mark followed Lamar's orders as he began to silently head back into Twan's bedroom with his tiny finger in his mouth innocently.

Twan and Lamar began to wipe their naked bodies off with their towels that laid to the floor,and as they were drying themselves from their steamy sexual encounter Deedra abruptly walked through the front door with grocery bags swinging from her hands.Twan quickly ducked his naked body to the floor behind the sofa to hide from Deedra as Lamar stood naked in Deedra's sight caught,his face guilty and in slight shock.Why it smell like all dick up in here,like somebody been fucking up in here,and why is it so damn hot?!

Deedra spoke as she fully entered the house and placed the bags on the counter softly.

What you just got out the shower? Deedra questioned Lamar in confusion as she saw him standing naked by the area rug with his towel swinging from his strong hand.Yea,i was about to go in the room before you came in,i just got out the shower,Lamar lied guiltily to Deedra as she stared at him with confusion,Deedra not fully believing his lie.

Let me see this towel,why you keep wiping your dick off like that,what you got something to hide? Deedra spoke to Lamar as she headed toward him,her face suspicious.

Naw,i was drying off,thats all man,Lamar spoke to Deedra nervously as she got closer to him.Let me see this motherfucking towel! Deedra snatched Lamar's towel from his hand as she began to study it carefully,her eyes examining a thick white substance on it.You then fucked somebody in this house,and then the bitch made you nut hard as fuck too,you dont even do that with me,Deedra spoke to Lamar with her nostrils flared in silent anger,Deedra knowing what exactly it was on Lamar's towel that he tried to hide from her.

Who the bitch you fuck tonight,she gone,or the bitch still up in here? Deedra spoke angrily to Lamar in a feeling of being betrayed.I aint fuck nobody man,stop accusing me of shit,Lamar spoke to Deedra.

Mark innocently exited Twan's bedroom and then began to speak softly to Deedra as she watched him from the left side of where she stood angrily.Lamar and cousin Twan were playing and Lamar peed on Twan,Mark informed Deedra in his chid voice,both Lamar and Twan's nerves nearly shooting through the roof at his informing Deedra of their sexual encounter.

He peed on Twan,boy what you talking about? Deedra spoke to Mark with confusion.This white stuff just shot out of Lamar's weewee on cousin Twan,and he and cousin Twan were naked,and he and Twan was crying and breathing really really hard,Mark spoke to Deedra as Deedra finally realized what exactly he meant,her eyes staring over at Lamar now,with hate.

Theres cousin Twan,i think now him and Lamar are playing hide and seek,i wanna play,Mark spoke to Deedra as he caught Twan ducking down naked and silent behind the sofa,Mark unknowingly telling on Twan and Lamar.

Twan stood up from behind the sofa with nervousness as he felt Deedra's eyes watching him and Lamar in disappointment.Lamar's towel fell from Deedra's hand as she stared both of them down in their nakedness in clarity and despair of what happened between them,Deedra giving Lamar the worst and longest stare of them all,the stare of a scorned lover.

Twan and especially Lamar learned that secrets sometimes became exposed,and sometimes exposed by things and people and little people you least expected.

The end

www.ingramcontent.com/pod-product-compliance
Lightning Source LLC
Chambersburg PA
CBHW030405290526
45785CB00004B/1911